The Sweetest Change

Michelle and her friends faced disappointment once again. It happened almost every week now. Whenever they wanted to go on a field trip, play a sport, or desired something new for their school, they always heard the same answer, "No, there's no money."

2

They were all so used to hearing that answer.

"When are we going to stop trying, guys?" Caleb insisted as always, "Even the teachers buy everything they need themselves. It's always going to be this way."

"Don't say that, Caleb," Tyler replied.

"Well, what are we going to do?" Nia asked.

"There's something we can do, guys," said Michelle with a smile. "Let's not give up. My dad always says that we can do anything we put our minds to. We can do something to fix it!"

"If the school hasn't found a way to get more funding, I doubt we'll ever find a way," Caleb said, but the smile on Michelle's face didn't go away.

That afternoon, Michelle thought long and hard, calculated, wrote, drew, and made plans. When her bedtime came, she was too excited to sleep. Michelle couldn't wait to tell her friends about her brilliant idea.

TABLET
FROG

The next day, Michelle ran to meet with the others as fast as she could.

"I got it. I got it!" She shouted when she saw them.

"What? What do you have?"

"I have an idea! I know how our school can have everything we want. Okay... ready? *A candy business.* It's simple. My mom loves to cook and bake, and she makes the best desserts in the world. We'll buy the ingredients, make the candy, and sell it at a higher price, earning enough to fix our school."

There was silence for a few seconds when Nia exclaimed, "That's brilliant! But how will we get the money, Michelle?"

Michelle smiled. "We'll put our money all together—our allowances, savings, money from birthdays. And we can ask our parents to donate some, too. That'll get us started and when we start to make a profit, we can pay them back!"

The others agreed it was a great idea, and they got to work.

Nia was an artist. So, she couldn't wait to get started on their business's sign. In just a day, she drew the best, biggest, most eye-catching sign. It had sparkles, lots of colors, and huge pictures of candies, cookies, cakes, and desserts of all kinds!

Caleb loved woodworking. He worked with his dad all the time. They made a stand for the desserts from some leftover wood they had lying around, and it looked great. "This will really attract people's attention," said Caleb. "Thanks for your help, dad!"

Tyler always had his head buried in books, so he did all the math and research. "Don't worry, I've got all the facts and figures, and I'll keep the books in order. We'll make a profit soon!"

COOKING

Michelle and her mom pulled all the cookbooks off the shelf and also got out their tablet computers. They looked and looked for all the best recipes for cookies, cakes, and candies. "Let's make sure the ingredients are affordable," said Mom. "That way you'll have more money left over, and you'll make a profit sooner."

Soon, they figured out what to make and got started. They pooled their money together and had just enough to buy everything they needed. At the store, they bought flour, sugar, and cocoa. They got chocolate chips, candy sprinkles, and even some wax paper.

Michelle and her mom, along with the kids, got to work baking. The kitchen was hot, flour was on the table (and a few faces!), but everyone was having so much fun.

When everything was ready, they taste-tested the desserts. Everything was so very delicious, just like Michelle said. Her mom was an expert!

And so, the very next day, Michelle and her friends set up their candy stand. "Great job, Caleb," said Michelle. "This stand is sturdy and big enough for all the candy and desserts."

According to Tyler's research, they picked the best place. There was always a ton of people in the park near their school. Kids played and ran around in the grass, and they always wanted candy.

As soon as Michelle and her friends put their stand down and set up the sign, a line of people waited their turn to try their candy, and the people weren't disappointed.

Michelle and Nia served customers, Caleb handled the money, and Tyler read a book, as usual. The candy sold out in just under an hour. They had enough to pay their parents back, buy the next batch of ingredients, *and* a bit left over.

CA$HIER
CANDY
SALE

Michelle and her friends couldn't have been happier. Soon, they packed it up and walked home.

"Hey, guys, it says here that if a product is in high demand, the prices go up," Caleb explained. "Everybody loved our candy, so I think we can raise our prices a little. For such a delicious product, I don't think our customers will mind."

Everyone thought it was a good idea. "Let's do it," said Michelle.

By the next day, everyone had heard about Michelle and her friends' business. Their entire school and neighborhood knew. Their neighbors stopped by to try their candy, and classmates came to help with the work. Even one local businessman came to help. He sold candy to big businesses and wanted to supply them with his best candy. Because of their noble cause, he gave the kids his candy practically for free. "I'm proud of each and every one of you," he said. "You remind me of myself at your age. You're learning how business works and you're giving back to your community!"

The business was booming. As more and more money came in, Michelle and her friends gave more to the school. One week, they got a vending machine, the next, they went on a field trip. Then came computers, learning games, toys, sports equipment, and whatnot. But that wasn't all!

The kids' entrepreneurial spirit inspired the whole school. Their friends and classmates came up with business ideas of their own and donated even more cool stuff to the school. The neighbors in the community wanted to help as well, so they donated some of their money to Michelle's school.

E-DEX

“I can’t believe it,” said Michelle. “It’s turned out even better than I imagined!”

“This is what happens when you do a good thing,” said her Mom brightly. “You attract people to your cause. And look how much you and your friends have learned.”

After a few months, the teachers had everything they needed, and the students had so much to do. They were all so happy to go to school, and their test results showed it. Having everything they needed, they learned more and became more focused.

At the end of the year, their school looked like a space station with all their futuristic technology. The teachers had big touchscreen boards to write on, tablets and computers were everywhere, and a drone delivered mail and flyers and made announcements.

Michelle and her friends couldn't believe how their small efforts could bring such a big change. With just an idea and a little bit of money, they helped themselves and others. And, they learned how to work as a team. Not only did they pool their money and resources together, but they each used their very own talents and skills to make their project a success.

SCHOOL

Michelle, Caleb, Nia, and Tyler became famous in their school and the entire city. Everyone heard of their creativity, selflessness, and generosity. In the long run, their small idea brought about a big change. Even after they graduated and moved on, little kids, just like them, heard of their heroics. Year after year they would come back to tell their story. They were all so very proud to make that contribution to their school and community. Although they created a successful business and plenty of money, they made sure the students knew that it's not about the money; it's what you do with it. Michelle, Caleb, Nia and Tyler will forever remember using their money to make The Sweetest Change.

THE END

Made in the USA
Middletown, DE
15 February 2021